The Ross of Mull Granite Qu

Margaret Mackinnon
Mull 1996.

The Ross of Mull Granite Quarries

The New Iona Press

ISBN 0 9516283 6 4

Cover design by David Faithfull
Front: painting of Tormore by William Caldwell Crawford (1879–1960).
Back: looking to Tormore from Tigh an Easbuig, Iona.
Inside front cover: Extract from Ordnance Survey map, 1885, sheet 43. Former quarry sites indicated. Reproduced by permission of the Trustees of the National Library of Scotland.
Inside back cover: Extract from map of Tormore area by William Sim, drawn 1860s. Reproduced by permission of the Argyll Estate Archives.
Unless otherwise acknowledged, photographs are from the author's family collection.

The publisher gratefully acknowledges subsidy from the Scottish Arts Council towards the publication of this volume.

Typeset by XL Publishing Services, Nairn
Printed in Great Britain
By Highland Printers, Inverness
For The New Iona Press
Registered address:
Old Printing Press Building,
Isle of Iona, Argyll PA76 6SL
Trading and correspondence address:
7 Drynie Terrace, Inverness IV2 4UP

Contents

Foreword 5
A Granite Landscape 7
Sources of the Stone 10
The Quarries at Work 14
Mull Granite Near and Far 29
Tormore Today 49
Appendix 52
Selected Sources 54

Foreword

My parents first came across the abandoned quarry houses at Tormore in 1926. They rented the upper row, which had been built as four two-roomed homes for the quarry workers, and in 1950 purchased them from the Duke of Argyll.

As children we loved to play in the quarries and climb on the piles of granite blocks and I can just remember the cranes and rails. We did hear stories about the old days – for instance, the late Charlie MacFarlane used to tell of the boys who one day released a truck at the top of the track and rode on it down to the pier, jumping off just before it plunged into the sea. We were also told that Neil MacCormick's house was buried under the top waste tip after he moved to Fionnphort. I only wish that I had asked more questions earlier.

It is not generally realised that there were as many as eight small quarries and that stone was also taken from many other parts of the tip of the Ross of Mull and its outlying islets. It is not always easy to tell whether rocks were felled by man or by nature, but it is interesting to look for clues such as cleft boulders, gaps, boreholes and squared-off blocks. Sometimes these are now concealed by bracken or seaweed.

Over the years there were occasional rumours that Tormore quarry might re-open. When it did, in 1986, my interest in its history was aroused in earnest as I watched the familiar outlines disappear. My observations and speculations link what I have been able to find in written sources with much of what I have heard. This story of the Ross of Mull quarries is inevitably incomplete, however. Exact dates and figures are at times elusive and there are often apparent contradictions. I would welcome any contributions or further information from readers.

Archivists and staff at the following places have been very helpful: Argyll Estate Archives, Inveraray Castle; Argyll & Bute District Archives, Lochgilphead; the Mull Museum, Tobermory; the Northern Lighthouse Board headquarters, Edinburgh; the Oban Times, Oban; the Royal Commission for Ancient and Historical Monuments of Scotland, Edinburgh.

Librarians from all over the country have kindly written in response to my enquiries, as have many individuals. I am particularly grateful to many people in the Ross of Mull who have generously shared information and memories with me during this research.

John Faithfull was responsible for the geology section and other members of my family have assisted in various ways. Most of all, I would like to thank Mairi MacArthur of the New Iona Press, whose help and encouragement have brought this book to completion.

Joan Faithfull

Former quarriers' cottages at Tormore, bought by William Crawford in 1950. The masonry detail at the top of page 5 shows the use of traditional lime seashell mortar.

A Granite Landscape

The granite end of the Ross of Mull extends to over twenty square miles of land, with a rocky, indented and sometimes steep coastline, sandy or stony beaches and many small outlying islands. The area stretches from just west of Bunessan, bounded by a line running between Camas na Criatha and Rudh Ardalanish, to the Sound of Iona and the Torran Rocks. From flat peaty moorland and cultivated patches, rise hillocks with almost as much rocky outcrop as vegetation. These are intersected by valleys and gullies, mostly running towards the sea but criss-crossed in places by other lines of rock face or by pathways.

Several early travellers and geologists wrote about the 'red' granite of Mull. It can appear almost red but is generally a pink of various shades, depending on its position, on whether it has weathered or been recently cleft, or if it is covered by lichen or washed by tides. Polishing, of course, gives the greatest and most lasting depth of colour. Sea-tumbled cobbles, plentiful on many stony beaches, are also smooth and clear in colour in contrast to the ice-borne boulders and other long-exposed surfaces which, although rounded, have a rough whitish-grey appearance.

The whole area is a rich natural source of hard, quality building material. To understand why, let us turn to how it was formed.

The granite in the Ross of Mull crystallised from molten magma intruded about 414 million years ago. This is about the same age as most of the other granites of mainland Scotland. The magma cooled a few miles underground on the north-western edge of a mighty mountain chain formed by the collision of two continental plates, rather like the Himalayas today. It was this collision which brought Scotland – then part of a continent with North America and Greenland – together with England and Wales, which at the time were joined to a large European–Scandinavian continent. Curiously, the boundary between these old continents is in almost exactly the same place as the Scotland–England border today!

The main constituent minerals of the rock can generally be seen with the naked eye: pink perthitic alkali feldspar (often called 'orthoclase'), creamy or white plagioclase feldspar, grey glassy quartz and small black biotite mica flakes. The pink colour of the alkali feldspar is caused by traces of iron and is due to an effect similar to rusting – when first formed it was probably grey or white. Smaller quantities of other minerals such as titanite, magnetite, pyrite ('fool's gold'), muscovite, hornblende, allanite, epidote, apatite and zircon also occur but you need very sharp eyes, or a microscope, to see them.

Although the rock is generally called 'granite', there are definite variations in composition and appearance in different parts of the outcrop. On Eilean a' Chalmain and around Cnocvuligan, in the south-west end of the Ross, you can see areas of dark grey rock, strictly called tonalite. These probably crystallised from the same magma as the main granite but were the very first rocks to form.

As the magma cooled and crystallised, it gave rise to rocks with less and less plagioclase and biotite, and more and more alkali feldspar and quartz. Thus the pink quartz-rich rock, such as that from Tormore, probably crystallised after the pale rock, such as that from Camas Tuath (North Bay). The very last dregs of magma to crystallise form thin, sub-horizontal 'veins' of rock cutting through the earlier-formed granite: fine-grained deep pink aplites and coarse-grained pink-and-white pegmatites. The former are quite common, the latter rather scarce but both can be seen on the west coast of Eilean nam Ban.

The granite is also cut by a variety of younger igneous rocks. The most obvious of these are the vertical, black basalt dykes. These are easily weathered and often form conspicuous gullies along coastal exposures of granite. The dykes are mostly much younger than the granite – only about 55–60 million years old! They are a nuisance from a quarrying point of view, as the granite is often fractured and altered near the dykes.

Where the granite has been in contact with acidic peaty water for a long time, it assumes a bleached white colour. The feldspars and mica are attacked by the water and form clay minerals and the rock tends to disintegrate, leaving a gravel of resistant quartz grains.

Polished Mull granite showing: 1 orthoclase (pink), 2 quartz (glassy), 3 biotite (black), 4 plagioclase (white).

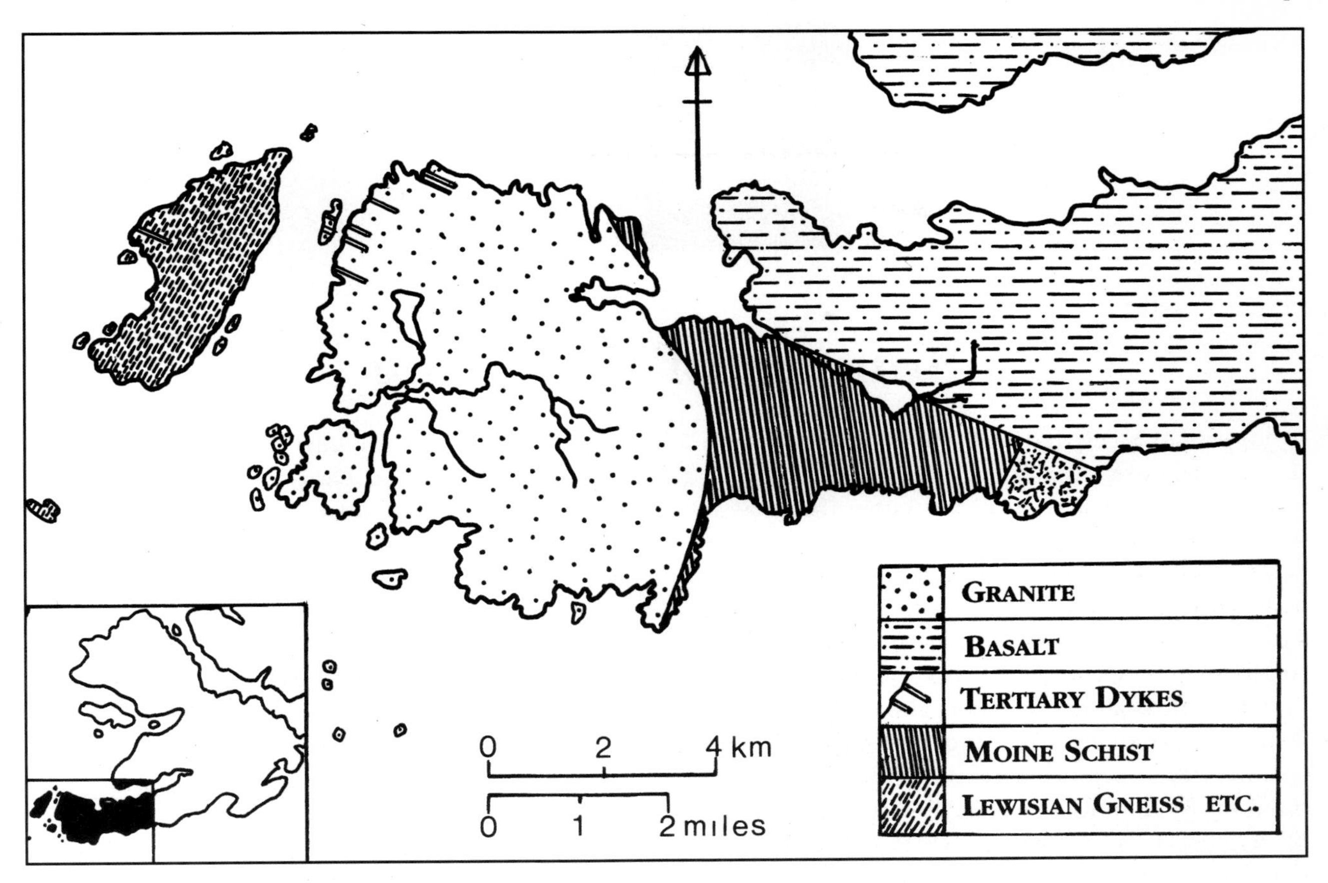

Geological map of the Ross of Mull.

Sources of the Stone

For ease of access and drainage, small quarries are generally worked into the sides of hills or cliffs or into the coast just above sea level, rather than downwards, although there will be masses of good stone below the quarry floor. The Ross of Mull granite quarries were typical of this pattern and, although small by mainland standards and remote, they were well known to Victorian engineers and architects.

The quality of the stone and particularly the availability of extremely large and flawless blocks was appreciated, as was the red colour and the lack of black knots. Thomas Telford, the Stevenson family of engineers, Sir George Gilbert Scott and Sir Charles Barry all chose Mull granite for some of their projects and many famous structures were wholly or partly built of it. Much also crossed the Atlantic.

Most of the granite sent away commercially for engineering and ornamental purposes went from the two largest quarries, the upper and lower levels at Tormore. Nearby were three small coastal quarries – each with its own jetty – at Deargphort, Eilean Dubh and Bull Hole. All, like Tormore, were sheltered to some extent by Iona and Eilean nam Ban.

A lot of stone from Deargphort, which was also called the Sound of Iona Quarry by its operator William Vass and which opened in 1871, was sold and sent for cutting and polishing to Aberdeen, Glasgow, Dalbeattie, Shap or Belfast to be made into small monuments.

The small Eilean Dubh – black island, also known as Vass's Island – faces Deargphort and should not be confused with nearby Eilean Dubh na Ciste. The Bull Hole Quarry is at Slochd na da Bhairnich, on the Mull shore of the main Bull Hole anchorage and opposite the north end of Eilean nam Ban. It has a very high face and there is clear evidence that a great deal of stone was taken away from there by sea. The only information traced about this quarry comes from an *Oban Times* report of 1886, which indicates that by then it had been closed for twenty years.

The two lighthouse quarries, at Erraid to the south and at Camas Tuath towards Bunessan, produced stone less red in colour than that from the coast and islands facing Iona. Camas Tuath translates as 'North Bay', the name by which it was always known to the Northern Lighthouse Board. This was the earliest site of quarrying on industrial lines, opened in 1839 for the building of Skerryvore Lighthouse.

At the north-eastern margin of the granite area, with quite deep sheltered water close to its low face, there was a small quarry at Rudh nam Bùthan – Booth Point – for the building of the new Baptist Church at Bunessan in 1890. Later there was an unsuccessful attempt to market this stone as 'Mull Grey'; it was the least pink of the Mull granites. A redder stone was also used in the church walls, making a deliberate and attractive pattern of contrast. Much earlier, stone had been taken from that point for a small shop on the sea-front, where the fire station now stands, to be built by Charles MacQuarrie, merchant in Bunessan. That is said to be how the point got its name.

There is a little quarry by the roadside, near the garage at Aridhglas, about two kilometres from Fionnphort, which provided stone for outhouses at Creich schoolhouse earlier this century. Later, during major road improvements on Mull in the 1960s a large crushing machine was imported and kept there, to produce road-metal from the granite.

Long before any of the quarries opened, a lot of surface stone was of course taken by local people for domestic purposes. The parish minister, writing in the *Statistical Account* of 1795, confirmed this: 'The whole coast of Ross, upon the Sound of Iona, is granite for several miles. No use is made of it, except

(*right, above*) Quarry at Deargphort, from the sea.
(*right*) Eilean Dubh quarry face and jetty.

in building farmhouses and walls'. The Duke of Argyll's instructions to his Chamberlain in 1801, relating to land division, included the note that tenants should each be given a sledge-hammer and 'crow-iron' for house and boundary construction.

On the geologically quite different island of Iona, erratics – granite boulders and cobbles of all sizes borne westwards during the last Ice Age – were plentiful on and in the ground. Stones were used whole for houses and march dykes, their rough surfaces holding together well without mortar while for the ecclesiastical buildings larger granite cobbles were split to give a flat face to inner and outer walls. Many Mull granite boulders are still to be seen on Iona, all along the east coast and particularly along the shore and on the grass to the north-east of the Abbey. Stone-masons building the small house at Clachanach in 1911 found all the material they required in the field between the road and that shoreline.

Across the water, St. Ernan's Church by the shore of Loch Poit I was built in 1899 of stone taken from a hillock behind the former Creich school, now the hall. Morag Maclean, whose eldest uncle was a quarry blacksmith at Tormore before emigrating to Canada, remembers watching Dòmhnall Phàraig – Donald MacCallum from Kentra – breaking boulders and hammer-dressing blocks at Caitchean in the late 1920s, for the new Fionnphort Post Office. Until well into this century, indeed, local stone was always used for building in the granite area of the Ross and it was often taken by sea to other parts of the island, such as Bunessan, Pennyghael and Tobermory.

On the Mull coast opposite the Bull Rock, where there is no quarry face, many very large boulders were deposited by glacier. Some show signs of boring and blasting and there is a small jetty. Exposed at low tide, lying forlornly on the rocks, is a shaped gravestone, clad in barnacles.

A navigation chart engraved in 1860 marks '18 foot stone' on the site of what later became the lower quarry at Tormore. This must be the same stone sketched by Henry Davenport Graham, author and illustrator of *Birds of Iona* who lived on Iona between 1848 and 1850. It shows himself looking at a very long stone and a note says: 'Near the top of a rugged little mount, an immense log of granite lies... upon the turf at Caitchionach Mòr. This is of red granite 18 foot long and is rounded on the upper side like a rude column... It was probably once set up on end'. We can only wonder today why it was there and what happened to it, but very probably it was split on the spot and the pieces taken away.

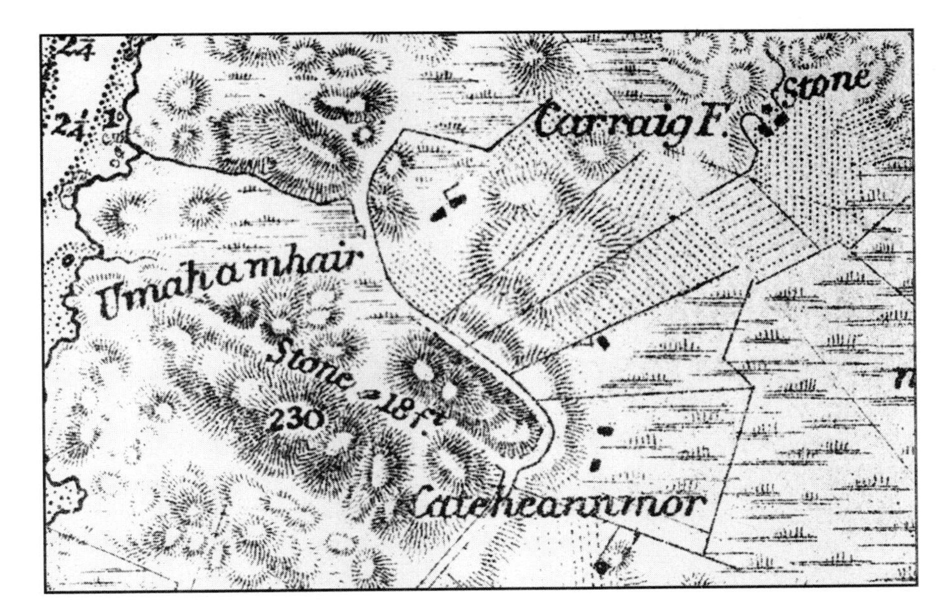

(left) Detail showing site of 18 ft stone from Admiralty chart 2617, 'Sound of Iona', surveyed by Commander E.J. Bedford, 1857–60.

(below) Drawing of 18 ft granite column from sketchbook of H.D. Graham, 1848–50. Courtesy of the Royal Commission on the Ancient and Historical Monuments of Scotland.

The Quarries at Work

The Rev Dr John Walker in his *Report on the Hebrides of 1764 and 1771*, recognised the potential of Mull's 'Red Granite':

> This stone was known to the Ancients by the name of Egyptian Porphyry, by the Italians it is called Granite rosso and by our English Antiquarians the Red Egyptian Granite… It is found in dispersed Masses in several parts of England and Scotland but in the Isle of Mull it is found in fast and extensive Rocks… Here the stone is to be had in as great Beauty and Perfection as any… Roman ruins in Italy. Blocks of it also are to be procured perfectly entire and of any Dimensions, and the quarries are upon the Sea Shore which would render the Transportation of the Stone easy to other Places.

This recommendation was echoed by another reputable figure, the German geologist Rudolph Erich Raspe who was invited by the Highland Society, presided over by the 5th Duke of Argyll, to make a mineralogical survey of the Highlands in 1789. In a letter to the Duke he reported:

> What I have chiefly to observe and say of these gigantic and romantic masses of granite is that in point of grain, texture, colour and hardness it is perfectly similar to the Egyptian granite Rosso Antico… It rises in this part of Mull in very large blocks… much superior to any I have seen in Cornwall… I am perhaps too warm and sanguine in my wishes and hopes to see these remote parts enlivened by useful industry.

Raspe's praise, in the same report, for the marble of Iona led directly to a short-lived commercial venture by the Duke at the Marble Quarry there. But it was to be another fifty years before Ross of Mull granite began to be worked in earnest by interests from outside the area.

It is difficult to give an exact or complete account of the management or finances of the Mull granite industry. Stone was taken from so many places, quarries opened and closed and opened up again depending on demand, and different companies, or sometimes the same companies under different names, operated over the years. Certain names, however, do recur in the records and these firms or individuals did have a definite involvement at various periods and they do seem to have co-operated with each other.

The **Northern Lighthouse Board** opened the North Bay quarry in 1839 and worked it until 1849 when it was taken over by Aberdeen architect and builder **William Leslie**. From 1832–1852 Leslie was also in partnership with Alexander MacDonald as MacDonald and Leslie, Monumental Sculptors, Aberdeen. MacDonald lived from 1794 to 1860 and was the founder of the Victorian polished granite industry in Britain, its most important figure and largest supplier of monuments. He was the first to use steam power for polishing stone and the machinery and tools he invented made the finished product inexpensive and then fashionable. The earliest polished granite memorials at Kensal Green and Highgate cemeteries in London were supplied by MacDonald & Leslie. Many later memorials would have been of Mull granite. MacDonald amassed a fortune and his son , also Alexander, was a major benefactor to Aberdeen Art Gallery and Museums.

William Leslie had already obtained the right to take stone from the coast and islands opposite Iona when appointed by the Duke of Argyll in the early 1850s to make repairs to Iona Abbey. About this time he was also shipping stone to Aberdeen for cutting and polishing and to Golspie for the Dunrobin Castle extensions (see p. 33). In 1853 he wrote to Argyll Estate Factor John Campbell about an order for Mull granite for a pier at Colonsay (see p. 33). Although in that year he had renewed a ten-year contract for North Bay, by 1857 other companies were showing interest in commercial quarrying in Mull and Leslie was asked to give up his lease. He seems to have relinquished it about this time.

Also in the late 1850s both **William Sim** and **Kirk Montgomery and Co**. of Liverpool were applying to the Duke and negotiating with his agent in Edinburgh, James Dalgleish. William Sim wrote in 1857: 'The quarries can only be opened up and wrought by the incurring of heavy expenditure on shipping, quays, railings etc which it would be hazardous to undertake without the positive certainty of continuous employment…'. He suggested a five year contract for 'the valley of Tormorchatton'. (This must be an anglicised combination of the hill name, Tòrr Mòr, and the adjoining township, Caitchean.)

Meanwhile, Kirk Montgomery & Co. had written in 1857 that 'demand at present is unlimited' and that they needed someone living on the spot to make decisions. They could finance the undertaking, which Sim may not have been able to do, and so they became the named tenants in partnership with Thomas Chaffer Esq., estate agents, surveyors and builders who owned quarries and cotton mills at Burnley and Nelson. The 12-year lease was for 'the shore from Slochd-an-da-Bharnich to Port na Mòna including the Island nam Bhan' [sic]. (Slochd na da Bhairnich is where the Bull Hole Quarry was sited.) A fixed annual rent of £75 was to be paid, along with Lordship (royalty) of 9d per ton on solid stone taken away. George Finch Montgomery also leased Fidden farm and shootings for several years.

Sim's relationship with the company is not clear,

but he appears to have worked with them in some capacity and he was certainly active in Mull over the same period. His home was Furnace Manse on Loch Fyne but he often visited the island. It was he who shipped a cargo of Tormore granite to Liverpool in 1857 to see if it would be acceptable for inclusion in the building of the docks, which it was. It was he who prepared the track for the rails at Tormore, laid later by manager James Spence, and he built the smiddy by the track and a powder-house above the quarry. And it was he who negotiated with A. Humbert, the Queen's architect, in 1862 concerning the use of Mull granite for the Royal Mausoleum at Frogmore in London.

Engraved portrait of William Sim, from the journal *The Bailie*, September 1886.

This energy is not surprising given William Sim's career up to that point. Born in 1814, he was the contractor for cleansing and lighting the streets of Glasgow when just 24 years old. Ideas for improving the city led him to Lochfyneside where, in 1841, he opened quarries at Furnace and Crarae to provide stone for paving setts. He became an expert on explosives, developing a method of detonating up to 60,000 tons of stone at one time. In 1855 Sim read a paper on 'The Quarrying and Blasting of Rocks' to the British Society for the Advancement of Science in Glasgow.

In 1862 the Illustrated *Oban Magazine & Argyllshire Advertiser* carried the news that: 'A prospectus has been issued of the Ross of Mull Granite Coy. with a capital of £50,000, in shares of £5 each. The object is to work on an extended scale...'. It went on to note that 'honourable mention has been awarded by the jurors of the International Exhibition to the Company for having opened up the fine red granite of that island'. This may have been a initiative by Sim on his own, or in conjunction with Kirk Montgomery, but in any case the latter seem to have withdrawn from Mull by about 1864.

St James Street
Glasgow
1st April 1862

Wm. Sim
to Duke of Argyll

My Lord Duke

I beg to inform your Grace that I have this morning received an order from Mr. A.S. Humbert, the Queen's Architect for the Royal Mausoleum to send to him with the least possible delay specimens of the Ross of Mull granite (pale red) to be submitted to the Queen.

1 *One specimen of N. Bay granite to be fine axed*
2 *One do. of N. Bay granite to be polished*
3 *One do. of ordinary red granite to be polished [Tormore]*
4 *One do deep coloured red granite to be polished [Tormore]*

Size 5½"–6" in length by 3¼" in breadth. Made in some form as paper weights polished on one surface and edges with particulars on paper Pasted on Back. I have dispatched an order to the Ross of Mull for the Stones to be sent me here per Islesman Steamer on Tuesday next. In case your Grace might also require one or more specimens I have provided to supply such.

Your most humble servant

William Sim

The Ross of Mull Granite Company then became part of the **Scottish Granite Company** of which William Sim had become a director along with George Muir who was another important figure in the story of granite. They had offices and polishing works in Glasgow and quarries at Bonawe as well as at Furnace and Crarae. James Spence acted as manager in Mull until 1867 when the 22-year old William Muir, son of George, was appointed. But by this time there were financial and practical problems which Muir was unable to rectify. The valuation roll for 1867/68 shows the company paying a rent of £258 for Tormore, a steep rise from the 1860 figure of £140, and the business may have become over-stretched. The company went bankrupt in 1868 and both the Mull leases and the Glasgow works were put up for sale. William Sim and the Scottish Granite Company continued to operate, however, but appear to have had no further direct involvement in Mull.

Between 1868 and 1871 there was little quarrying in the area except at Erraid, where many men were employed extracting and preparing stone for Dhu Heartach lighthouse. (See p. 42) Some lived on Erraid but others were prepared to walk there every day, over considerable distances, for work. Attie MacKechnie's grandfather Donald MacGillivray went from Ardalanish, for example, and Hersey and Mary MacFarlane's grandfather Duncan MacFarlane walked from Creich.

In 1871 **J. & G. Fenning** of the Shap quarries in Westmoreland took over at Tormore, opening the upper quarry. The polishing machinery was transferred from Glasgow to the Shap site where much stone was later sent, going by sea to Silloth on the Solway Firth and thence by rail. William Muir came back as manager and Neil MacCormick, a local man, became the foreman. North Bay was also included in Shap's lease.

The names of Muir and MacCormick are closely intertwined in the local history of the Ross of Mull. **William Muir** was born in Glasgow in 1845. His father George W. Muir was an engineer who wrote a long and interesting article for the *Journal of Practical Mechanics* in 1866. He mentioned the Scottish Granite Company 'with which I am connected' and this link must have led to his son's first, short-lived employment on Mull in 1867-68. On William's return, to work for Fenning's, he built a handsome home, large for its day, overlooking Fionnphort bay. It was known as Tormore House and then as Fionnphort House. Unfortunately, it burnt down in the 1950s and the stone was removed by the Iona Community for their rebuilding work. The present ferryman's house stands on the site.

William Muir made many friends in Mull and became particularly close to the family of Neil MacCormick, his foreman. When Muir left the island in 1875 there was a farewell dinner for him in Bunessan Hotel. He went south to Manchester and then London but the Mull connection was by no means severed. In the capacity of 'granite agent', he shared offices with granite merchant D.D. Fenning, of the Shap family, and they continued to deal with Tormore granite. In 1883 they both moved to the premises of Jabez Druitt, stone merchant and monumental mason.

William Muir married Miss Sophia Druitt and settled down in East London. He shared with that family a great admiration for the work and artistry of William Blake. In 1884 Muir began his most ambitious project, the production of hand-made facsimiles of the poet's *Prophetic Books* using, as far as he could rediscover them, the original techniques of Blake himself. The Druitt sisters coloured the facsimiles by hand. This interest continued for the next thirty years and the works are nowadays highly considered by Blake scholars and collected by enthusiasts, particularly in the USA.

This spare-time enthusiasm led to another link with the MacCormick family – the establishment of The Iona Press in 1887, housed in a bothy opposite the island's St Columba Hotel. Muir directed the venture, mostly at a distance, and enlisted John MacCormick, eldest son of Neil, as on-the-spot printer and binder. They published around a dozen pamphlets of Gaelic poems and prayers, hand-coloured by local girls in the style of the Blake Press, and also a *Life of St Columba* by Muir himself.

Meanwhile William Muir's main employment as granite agent continued until at least 1902 and one of his most influential customers was Count Gleichen, a sculptor and a nephew of Queen Victoria. Mull granite was probably used for many plinths and steps beneath Victorian statues.

Neil MacCormick succeeded William Muir as Tormore quarry manager in 1875 and moved into Fionnphort House with his wife Annabella MacLachlan and their large family, of eventually eleven. Neil had been born in Iona in 1836 and shortly afterwards the family moved across to the Ross of Mull. He worked in the quarries from an early age, acquiring great knowledge and technical skill. It is said that his invention of a brake, applied by a lever, to the steep rail which took trucks from the upper Tormore quarry down to the quay became widely known. A memorable event in his life was a visit to Egypt to advise in a dispute about transport methods which had arisen between the Government there and a firm of London sculptors who had leased a large porphyry quarry.

Neil MacCormick took a close interest in the social and religious life of the community. Besides leading the local choir, he was a precentor in the Free Church and was president of the Band of Hope (later the Temperance Society) which met once a fortnight at Creich School and to which William Vass and quarrymen such as Lachlan MacCormick and Alexander Maclean also belonged. Neil also liked sailing and competing in regattas with his boat the *Fairy Queen*. Two months before his death in 1925, at the ripe old age of 90, he and Brigadier General Cheape judged the piping competition at the Iona Regatta and Games. A tribute to his memory in the *Oban Times* of 21 November 1925 was fittingly headed 'A Noted Highlander'.

Fenning's quarrymaster in 1871 was **William Vass** who had first come to Mull in the early 1840s as a quarrier at North Bay. He was away from the island during the 1850s but had returned by 1861 when the Census lists him living at Ardfenaig, not far from North Bay, and working as 'overseer of granite quarry', presumably for William Sim's outfit. During the short gap after the Scottish Granite Company's collapse Vass remained on Mull and may have already been operating independently. He certainly kept aware of market demand, writing to the Argyll Estate factor in September 1869: 'Messrs. Newall of Dalbeattie promised they would take seven cargoes, Mr. Mossman of Glasgow would take two cargoes… in all 17 cargoes yearly. There are a few more polishers I know would take the red granite if I ship them under Peterhead prices… 2/9 per cubic foot'.

By 1871 it seems that besides acting as quarry-master for Fenning, Vass had opened his own Sound of Iona Quarry at Deargphort which employed 34 men initially and lasted until 1882. Another small Vass quarry on Eilean Dubh continued a little longer.

By the early 1880s there was some fluctuation in demand which in turn led to ups and downs for the local workforce. On 15 May 1886 the *Oban Times* reported:

> The Ross of Mull quarries once gave employment to many men. Bull Hole quarry stopped about 20 years ago, Deargphort stopped four years ago but paid all its workers. Tormore ceased more than a year ago, causing much destitution; the Eilean Dubh quarry is still carrying on and paying the workmen every Saturday evening.

Earlier that year, in February, the paper had reported good prospects for Eilean Dubh owing to the 'superior quality' of its stone but that Mr. Vass, the operator, had considerable practical problems to contend with working from a small offshore island in the frequently cold and stormy weather.

Vass's involvement in the quarrying business was long and, although he was a native of Logie-Easter in Ross-shire, his name had become firmly identified with Argyll by the time he died in Oban in 1896, at the age of 78. His obituary in the journal *The Quarry* made this clear in May of that year:

> It is with profound regret that we record the death of Mr. William Vass, one of the best known quar-

rymasters of Scotland. We have said 'of Mull' because... from his association with the celebrated granite that crops out at Bunessan we refuse to imagine him as living elsewhere. ... He was first engaged by the Northern Lights Commissioners for work at Skerryvore and Sanda lighthouses. It is nearly 50 years since he opened the island quarry at Bonawe and he set the first blast at the Cruachan granite quarries in the Loch Awe region. He also opened five granite quarries in the Ross of Mull and while under his management he quarried and shipped granite for [many] structures and buildings... He also supplied many Iona crosses, one of which was for the last Duchess of Argyll and one for the late Duchess of Westminster.

William Vass's first wife was Jane Livingstone from Kentra and they had six children. The three eldest sons were to become stone-masons with the third one, Alexander, making a name for himself as a monumental sculptor in Oban. When Jane died in 1872 she was buried in the old Kilpatrick graveyard near Bunessan, beneath a handsome Mull granite obelisk erected by her husband and sons. William remarried and had more children and both he and younger members of the family are buried at Pennyfuir near Oban.

By 1889 Fennings' financial troubles had grown to such an extent that they had to give up in Mull. Aware of this, another company – the Ulster Granite, Marble and Stone Works – wrote to the Duke of Argyll:

We have been using and manufacturing for a number of years past small quantities of red granite from Mull, some of which we obtained from Messrs. Fenning of Shap and some from Mr. Vass, Sound of Iona. We understand the quarries at Tormore are now in Your Grace's possession and that there is still a quantity of material on the ground...

Oban Times, 8 February 1873
Screw steamer *Albert* arrived on Monday loaded with a cargo of granite blocks from Tormore quarry. Proceeding south on Tuesday.

Oban Times 16 January 1892
The steamer *Inniemore* loaded a consignment of granite at the new quarry Booth Point near Bunessan. The stone is to be sent to the company's monumental works at Shap. The colour is grey, fine in grain, hard and takes a fine polish.

They asked if they could purchase the quarried stone. The Duke's response is not known but in any case, two years later in 1891 the Fennings renewed their interest in Tormore, taking a lease under the name of the **Shap Granite & Concrete Company**.

Business carried on spasmodically until around 1907. Although the middle of 1899, for example, was busy, with a shipment of 140 tons destined for the Kirklee Bridge in Glasgow, *The Quarry* had reported earlier the same year that work had been suspended in Mull due to 'slackness of trade' and that 'the place was jammed up with accumulated stock'. Such erratic demand must have made operating very difficult and did cause local hardship, even resentment. The Free Church minister in the Ross, the Rev. William MacMillan, had written to the *Oban Times* in February 1885 to bring to public notice 'the very trying circumstances of the people in this part'. He claimed that the quarries had not been run satisfactorily and that many were now 'cast adrift in a penniless condition without any prospect of work'. There were complaints too from crofters about the letting of crofts and part of the common grazing to the quarry and about restriction of access to their stock watering-place by new quarry dwellings.

In 1901 a company at Cefn-y-Wern in North Wales had made a move to take over both the Mull and Shap quarries but nothing came of this. In 1910, however, a Liverpool company calling itself the **Ross of Mull Granite Quarry Company** did take over the Tormore lease, intending to introduce new working methods and to give regular local employment. Unfortunately, these hopes were not fulfilled. Imports of cheap foreign granite had led to a decline in the native industry, while changes in taste and fashion, plus the widespread use of reinforced concrete, made recovery even more difficult. By 1913 a great deal of quarry-dressed stone and machinery lay abandoned. The following year most of the erstwhile workforce was called to war.

Some of the quarrymen and their families, who lived in company properties, were allowed to stay on when the operations ended. But the long period of well over half a century, when work at one or other of the quarries was usually in prospect, was finally over.

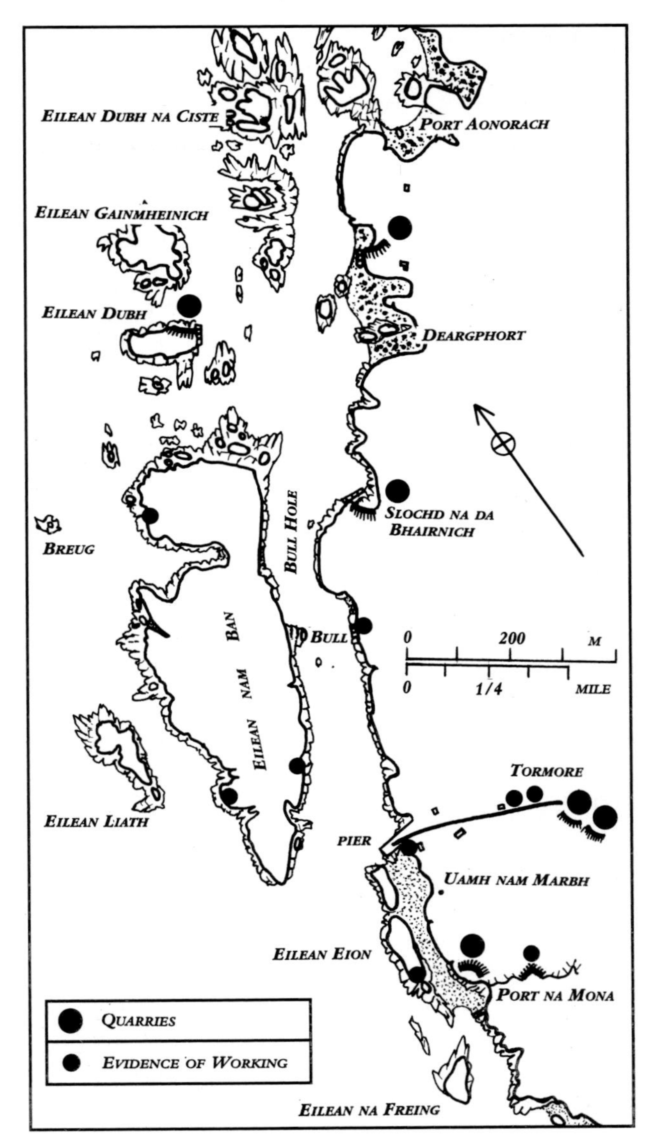

Area of quarrying activity between Fionnphort and Kentra

Working and moving the stone

Different methods of extracting and splitting granite were used over the years. One of the earliest, known as fire-setting, was described in the 1939 *Geological Survey of Great Britain*: 'The old technique survives in the Outer Hebrides of breaking [granite] boulders by building fires upon them and quenching with cold water'. In *My Life of Song* Marjory Kennedy Fraser writes that she saw this in the Outer Hebrides in the 1930s. And Donald MacDonald's book *Lewis. A History of the Island* includes a photograph from the Scottish Ethnology Archive captioned: 'Splitting boulders by heat for house-building and road-making, 1938'. No account referring directly to Mull or Iona has been found but this procedure might well have been employed there at one time.

Another early method of splitting granite was to insert dry wood plugs into a line of small shallow-bored holes and then to soak them with water until the wood expanded, causing a block or boulder to divide. In a similar way, the plug-and-feather technique was and still is used. Two feathers (strips of iron) are placed opposite each other in each of a row of holes varying from finger size and four inches apart to much larger and farther apart. Short tapered iron plugs are placed between the feathers and hammered in successively until even large masses will split cleanly. These processes must not be hurried.

Two brothers from Kentra, Peter and Duncan MacCallum, became particularly well known in the district during the late nineteenth century for their stone-mason skills and Peter's son Donald and Duncan's son John carried the craft on into this century. Early quarry work was entirely dependent on manual labour as cranes, drills and all tools were operated by hand. Steam power does not seem to have been used on the Ross of Mull, although it was used on Dhu Heartach rock in the late 1860s and in the larger mainland quarries.

For blasting and dividing rock an understanding of the directions of cleavage is necessary. The nature of most granite assists man to form rectangular blocks of it, as natural separations parallel the directions of easiest splitting which are known as the 'rift' and the 'grain' or 'reed'. The rift is generally vertical and at right angles to the grain while the third dimension , known as the 'hardway' has no particular direction of fracture. Main lines of boreholes must follow either rift or grain.

Black powder (gunpowder) was preferred to dynamite for blasting, being less drastic and easier to control. Nevertheless, a great deal of skill and experience was required to assess the right quantity. Too much could cause unwanted shattering, while too little was ineffective and wasteful. On Mull huge tunnels and 'monster blasts' were not employed, as they were on the Argyll mainland, since the main requirement was for large dimension stone with as little waste as possible. Powder-houses were needed to secure explosives.

Boreholes for blasting were generally made downwards, but occasionally horizontally using a jumper, a long heavy iron bar with a chisel end. This was held in place and turned round slowly by one man while two others struck it alternately with sledge hammers. From time to time water was poured into the hole and the sludge removed with a scraper. A leather collar prevented the holes from becoming triangular. About a hundred blows made a hole about two and a half inches deep and of the same

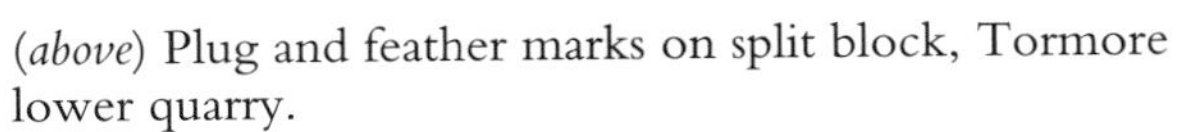

(*above*) Plug and feather marks on split block, Tormore lower quarry.

(*above, right*) Boulder on shore opposite Bull Rock, prepared for splitting with wedges.

(*right*) Jumper still in quarry face, Tormore lower level.

diameter

Some jumpers had two chisel ends and a heavy iron ball at the centre of the shaft to add weight. These were used by one man standing on the stone, holding the tool with one hand above and one under the knob, turning and plunging it up and down on the spot where the hole was to be. Rusty remains of jumpers have been found at Tormore, including a part which was mistaken for a cannon ball. Boreholes are visible on quarry faces, some more than eleven feet long.

Blacksmiths were frequently required to sharpen and temper tools and to repair lifting chains etc. Smiddies, now roofless, can be seen at Tormore, Erraid and Camas. Wells are close by and, beneath turf and bracken, are mounds of clinker which is now combined with soil like currants in a cake.

Houses in the Ross of Mull were often built from nearby outcrops of suitable rock, natural 'joints' of which could be levered out and divided up. Some of these joints or posts were enormous but there were, and are, many vertical man-sized sections which could be extracted for subsequent splitting. They were levered outwards and down by pinch (a crowbar) while increasingly large stones were dropped in behind to prevent them tipping back to their original positions. This method could be used in quarries too when natural divisions made blasting unnecessary. Blocks prised or blasted from the Mull coast and from Eilean nam Ban were taken by sea to Iona or to non-granite parts of Mull.

The quarries needed cranes for lifting and shifting. These would have been Scotch Derricks – vertical pivot posts swivelling in heavy rock bases, supported by three timber legs, and with long, angled jibs. Some remains of rusty old winches can be seen at Deargphort quarry and on the beach when the tide is low at Camas. One on Tormore pier is almost complete and incorporates stumps of massive 12 × 10 inch timber. There is also a pivot block measuring 6ft × 6ft × 18ins and the stacked blocks of stone which anchored the legs are still in position. This was a huge derrick, looming over the pier.

Up the hill, at the top of the steps, rests a heavy bell which was part of the upper quarry crane which, until about 1930, could be seen from Iona, clearly silhouetted against the sky. On Erraid pier, the working platform included a travelling crane on rails.

Inland, where there were no rails, horse-drawn slipes (sledges) were probably used on fairly level

Crane on Tormore pier, 1920s.

ground as were rollers and perhaps two and four-man hods or hand barrows. An account in the *Oban Times* of 6 February 1892 gives a vivid description of the loading process at Tormore, from upper quarry to waiting vessel, and includes mention of Neil MacCormick's rail brake :

> Tormore boasts of the best granite in all Scotland, its rival being Peterhead. The quarry is on the face of a high hill rising in terraced gradients from the Sound of Iona. The pier is about 700 yards from the quarry and the ingenious manner – the invention of the present manager – in which the

(*right*) Looking from Tormore to Eilean nam Ban and Iona. In the foreground, remains of the bridge under which ran the main tramway. (*below*) Rails in place, 1920s; former smiddy on the right.

> wrought granite is brought down the steep rails is both surprising and interesting.

It goes on to describe the steeper slope leading down from the quarry as forming an angle of 145 degrees at the bottom and bearing a double row of narrow gauge rails. The waggons were controlled by 'staunch iron chains' wound round a huge iron drum, the stone base of which can still be seen at the top of the steps. When one waggon was let go with its load of up to 20 tons of granite, its weight pulled an empty one up. The observer continues :

> The drum is worked by a brake and the whole operation is done with the correctness of clock-work. When the loaded waggon comes to the foot of the steep incline, the stone is transferred to the shipping waggon, a strongly built crane being erected at the foundation for this purpose. As soon as the shipping waggon receives its cargo the driver adroitly grasps the long iron lever, lifts it slightly upwards and away goes the waggon at its 10 mph pace with half a dozen workmen perched on top of the stone.
>
> In rainy weather, when the rails are slippy and braking is not easy, the men find their seats rather irksome as the waggon is apt to run away. To counteract this, however, sand is spread on the rails... a good deal of care and skill is applied and mishaps are few and far between. As soon as the load of granite is shipped the empty waggon is pulled up by two hardy Highland ponies and the operation is repeated until the steamer at the pier is down to the Plimsoll mark and then the full cargo is registered.

Abandoned winch on Tormore pier

The writer also noted that the stones varied in weight from two hundredweight to 12 or 15 tons. Although it was not practical to weigh the stone on site, measurement provided an estimate of weight.

Disposing of unwanted stone was always a problem. From Tormore, for example, only dimension stone (large rectangular blocks) was exported. Almost all the stone was of sound quality but squaring-off provided masses of waste. It has never been used for road-building, except locally, not being suitable for street setts nor for commercial crushing.

There was once a bridge over the main tramway, supported by tall well-built walls which have survived. It bore rails taking waste away from the lower quarry to the north-east. Several long, flat-topped spoil tips – formed as irregular, unwanted

Columns of Mull granite in Kirklee Bridge, Glasgow.

Ruined house and walls of local granite, between Kentra and Deargphort.

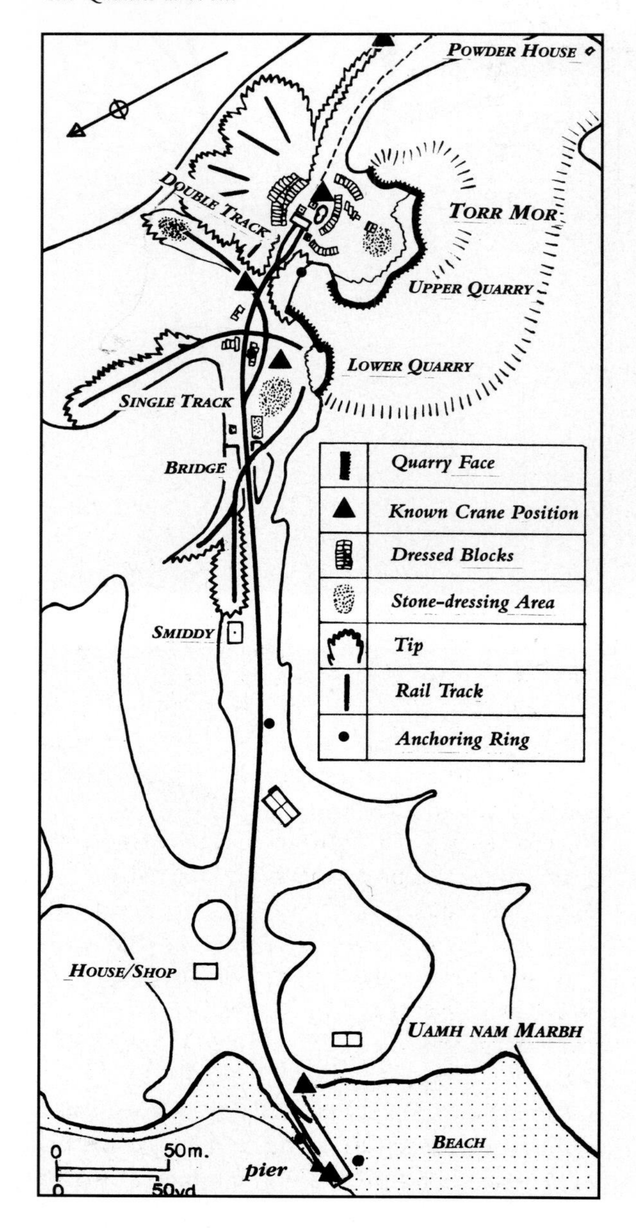

blocks were tipped sideways from small man-handled trucks – radiated from both quarries. Many of these waste blocks have recently been taken to support planned road improvements along Loch Scridain and for the new bus-park extension at Fionnphort. After the earlier quarrying stopped, some of the rails were taken for slipways or for supporting small bridges locally. During the Second World War the rest were then lifted and piled on the pier to be shipped away for salvage. In the 1950s scrap merchants were permitted to remove most of the old machinery from the Tormore quarries.

(*left*) Map of locations within Tormore quarries, as they were during the period of operation.
(*above*) Remains of powder house, Tormore; to its right is a typical granite outcrop.

Mull Granite Near and Far

According to Dr. John Walker in 1744, granite was 'the fittest material in the world for monuments' and this was indeed one of the main uses to which the Mull stone was put.

In 1866 the 8th Duke of Argyll raised a memorial to his great ancestor Sir Colin Campbell, Cailean Mòr, who had been slain in battle in 1294. This massive horizontal slab of Mull granite is in Kilchrennan old burial ground and bears in relief a large antique sword. It had been cut, polished and inscribed at Aberdeen by McDonald, Field & Company.

In 1882 , by permission of the Duke of Argyll, a handsome granite obelisk was erected by the US Government in the Reilig Odhrain in Iona, to commemorate American sailors drowned in the wreck of the *Guy Mannering* in 1865. And in 1879 the Duke raised a tall Celtic cross in memory of his first wife Elizabeth Sutherland. Sometimes known as 'Vass's Cross' it stands by the roadside north of Clachanach croft, looking over to the quarries where William Vass and many others hewed the stone over the years. Stone for a similar cross was furnished by Vass for Elizabeth's sister the Duchess of Westminster, who died in 1880 aged only 28. Inscribed in both Gaelic and English, it stands on an island in Loch Stack in Sutherland.

From about 1870 until the end of the century we do know that both William Vass and Neil MacCormick were sending loads of stone to agents such as Fenning and William Muir in London and to granite merchants in Aberdeen, Glasgow, Dalbeattie (Newall & Co.) and Belfast (John Robertson & Co.). This was mainly for monumental purposes – memorials, columns and plinths.

We know also that Mossman, the well-known Glasgow monumental sculptors, bought cargoes of Mull granite during the 1870s. And Alexander Vass, third son of William and Jane, was a monumental sculptor in Oban for many years. He was responsible for numerous gravestones in the area, some with the incised 'signature' VASS on the right-hand side of the base.

Celtic crosses of Mull granite can also be seen at Pennyfuir cemetery, Oban and at Pennygown and other cemeteries on Mull. Another popular form of memorial was a headstone with an obelisk set above it. An example of the latter is over the grave of Neil MacCormick, quarry manager, buried in Iona.

Lettering inscribed on Mull granite does not always show up well even on polished surfaces, so in-filling with paint or the application of metal letters is advisable. Some old granite gravestones on Mull and Iona were cut and dressed locally and are very hard to read. Beneath one of these, at Old Kilpatrick on Mull, lies the quarryman Andrew Munro who came from Easter Ross in 1840 to work at North Bay and who died on the island in 1854 but his epitaph is now scarcely decipherable owing to the rough crystal and lichen.

The 8th Duke of Argyll was a keen amateur geologist, and Fellow of the Royal Society, and he liked the granite from his estate to be used and seen. When the Oxford University Museum was completed in 1860 it contained many interior Gothic pillars of native marbles and granites, carefully labelled as specimens. Of these the Duke of Argyll had presented two, one of Mull granite and the other from Loch Fyneside, both polished in Glasgow. Of about twenty different granites displayed, nine are Scottish, one is from Jersey and the rest are from Cornish quarries.

Another example of Mull granite survives in the Hunterian Museum in Glasgow. It consists of a rough base, a dressed plinth and a short polished column and was one of four samples, two of different shades from Mull and two from Shap in Westmorland, given by stone merchant D.D. Fenning to the City Industrial Museum, Kelvingrove Park in 1876. Today the Hunterian Museum displays a large chunk of Tormore granite recently presented by Scottish Natural Stones Limited.

Mull granite sample presented by Fenning, 1876. Now at the Hunterian Museum, Glasgow.

(*above, left*) Monument to Lord Colonsay, Isle of Colonsay; (*above, right*) granite columns on the Argyll Car Factory building, Alexandria; (*right*) Hynish Pier, Tiree, built of North Bay granite.

Iona

The best known and oldest examples of the local use of Mull stone are to be found on Iona. The medieval Christian buildings there are mainly of granite, either obtained from the erratics left by ice or from blocks brought over from the Mull coast by boat. In writing about his famous journey to the western islands in 1773, Dr. Samuel Johnson described their approach to Iona: 'We were very near an island called the Nuns' Island, perhaps from an ancient convent. Here is said to have been dug the stone which was used in the buildings of Icolmkill'. There are no signs of Eilean nam Ban ever having been inhabited but it can be seen that much stone was taken from its steep coast.

On her way to Iona in 1802, having ridden across Mull, Mrs. Sarah Murray sat on her horse '... dumb with amazement, occasioned by the huge fantastical rocks of fine red granite, similar to the Egyptian, standing and lying in every imaginable form all along the Mull shore for miles'. She also stated, probably rightly, that women only lived occasionally if at all on Eilean nam Ban, describing it as '...a rugged huge mass of red granite, without any appearance of soil. ...I was told that from the Island of Women came all the stone with which the buildings at Iona were constructed.'

The Rev. Donald Campbell, parish minister, recorded in the *New Statistical Account* of 1842/43:

> [The Abbey] is extremely remarkable for the materials of which it is constructed, being built of sienite or red granite brought from the opposite coast of Mull. There the stone is procured in abundance and of the best quality, equal indeed to the famous red granite which the Romans brought from upper Egypt with which they erected their most superb monuments. It is nowhere polished in any part of the building but painfully formed, by hammering, to a plain surface; and there are many fine blocks of it, five or six feet long, both in the walls and in the rubbish. ... The rock is solid, the stone of almost impenetrable hardness.

The Nunnery, St Ronan's Church, St Oran's Chapel and the Abbey with its surrounding buildings all have attractive masonry in which different shades of pink granite dominate. In a field to the north-east of the Abbey the tall remaining wall of Tigh an Easbuig (the Bishop's House) stands firm on earthfast boulders, its various stones bonded with hard lime mortar.

Not many of Iona's carved antiquities are of granite but one horizontal dressed slab of Mull granite still lies in the Reilig Odhrain. On it is carved a large ringed cross and it is traditionally believed to have covered the tomb of an unnamed French king. Outside the west door of the Abbey is a long block of granite with a small incised Greek cross at one end and a shallow carved depression forming a trough in which pilgrims washed their feet.

St Martin's and St Matthew's crosses (8th–10th centuries) were inserted into rounded, stepped bases of granite, probably carved a few centuries later. Another similar but empty pedestal can still be seen outside St Oran's Chapel.

The parish church and manse on Iona, designed by Thomas Telford, were built of Mull granite in

1828. The front and sides of the church show measured rectangular stones laid in level courses and must surely be the earliest example of ashlar building in the area, erected ten years before Skerryvore lighthouse was begun. Later notable granite buildings on Iona include the Bishop's House, designed by Inverness architect Alexander Ross and completed in 1894, and the local library built by Fletcher of Tobermory in 1904.

Colonsay

The original pier at Scalasaig was built of the local hard dark diorite rock. Between 1850 and 1853 it was considerably extended, using North Bay granite. An unusual rounded breakwater was built on the other side of the bay, of both the diorite and the more easily worked Mull granite, supplied by William Leslie. David Stevenson and Alan Brebner were responsible and the Fishery Board paid £2,981 for the work.

On Cnoc na Faire Mòr, prominent above the bay, is a 30 foot high obelisk of pink granite in memory of Duncan MacNeill, Lord Colonsay (1793–1874). It bears a lightning conductor – and for good reason. Only sixty-three days after the memorial was inaugurated on 9th August 1876, in the presence of nearly 300 inhabitants most of whom had contributed to its cost, it was struck by lightning. The pedestal, on three sides of which were inscriptions in English, Gaelic and Latin, was severely damaged. The obelisk itself survived and was later set onto a new base bearing a much simpler inscription.

The original monument was supplied and erected by William Vass of the Sound of Iona Granite Quarries. Pieces of the first pedestal were later used for various purposes in the island; for example, pink granite quoins – with some words still visible in three languages – are built into Ben Odhran House.

Also of Mull granite are two large blocks covering the bodies of the 3rd Baronet Strathcona and his wife in Kilchattan graveyard. In the grounds of Colonsay House, concealed by foliage, are other bits of pedestal and some of the stone is in the garden of the Isle of Colonsay Hotel.

Dunrobin Castle

Well before the main quarry was opened, stone was taken from around the beach near Tormore. At its southern end, at Port na Mòna, a simple quarry face with a vertical bore mark, can still be seen and this provided stone for the extensions and alterations to Dunrobin Castle, completed in 1852. Later, in 1869, William Sim sent a sketch map of the Tormore quarries to the Duke of Argyll. It included the words 'stone for Dunrobin Castle' marked at Port na Mòna. (See map, inside back cover).

The Aberdeen architect William Leslie, along with Sir Charles Barry, was responsible for the improvements at Dunrobin. He seems to have preferred the pinker granite of the Tormore area, rather than the North Bay stone, for the castle. It may seem strange that granite should have been shipped from the west coast to the east when there was so much available around Aberdeen and Peterhead. Mull is near the Loch Linnhe end of the Caledonian Canal, however, and Golspie is not very far from the Inverness end. Later, a great deal of stone from Tormore and Deargphort was shipped to Aberdeen.

(*above left*) pillars below Holburn Viaduct, London; (*left*) Mull and Italian granite form an attractive pattern on the floor of the Trustee Savings Bank, George Street, Edinburgh; (*above*) Friends at the unveiling of the memorial to Eric Liddell, Shandong Province, China, June 1991.

London

The Albert Memorial

One of the most famous and spectacular monuments in the world, the Albert Memorial in Kensington Gardens, must also be the best-known structure to have incorporated Mull granite. Unfortunately, internal water seepage has made it unsafe and for the last ten years the memorial has been hidden and guarded by what is thought to be the largest free-standing scaffold in Europe, encased in plastic. Only recently has a decision been made to proceed with repairs, the estimated cost of which has risen to £13 million. It is hoped that by the end of the century the monument will have emerged, sound and brighter than ever.

Things would have been different had Queen Victoria's original idea been carried out. When Prince Albert died in 1861 she had wanted an enormous granite obelisk to be erected in his memory. George Gilbert Scott designed one to be set on an elevated granite platform with four crouching lions at the corners. On the sides of the granite obelisk would have been carved scenes from Albert's life and its apex would have been capped with metal and a magnificent Iona-style cross.

A huge, almost horizontal monolith was selected on the side of the hill to the north-east of Tormore. It would have weighed about 700 tons and we may wonder now whether it would have been possible to remove such a stone intact from the hillside and transport it whole to London, but Mr. George Muir of the Scottish Granite Company seems to have been undaunted. When the overlying stone was removed, however, a flaw came to light and the project was abandoned. Ever since, it has been known as 'the Prince's Stone' and can still be seen, with boreholes visible in the felled overlay.

In London it was then decided to hold a competition for a different kind of monument and the winning design, also by George Gilbert Scott, was for a huge flamboyant Gothic revival temple, 175 feet high, with a statue of Albert and many other sculptures. It took nine years to build, from 1863 to 1872, and earned its architect a knighthood. It has always been an object of controversy, having been described both as an: '... embarrassing example of the vulgar ostentation of Victorian Gothic' and '... the greatest single work of the Gothic revival of Architecture in Britain'.

Queen Victoria laid its first stone in May 1863. Many highly skilled engineers, stone-masons and sculptors were employed. Many different materials were carefully selected, including over 12,000 mosaic pieces. Enamelling and gilding ensured a brilliant effect. Granites from Ireland, Cornwall and the Aberdeen area as well as from Mull were used for colour contrast, both polished in the higher parts and unpolished lower down. Marble and other stones were also required. On the site was machinery for cutting, dressing, turning and polishing. Conspicuous, and enclosed by bands of bronze and gems, are the clusters of red Tormore and grey Castwellan (Irish) granite columns supporting the tall ornate canopy above the once gilded statue of Albert. Also of Tormore granite are some of the many plinths, platforms and panels.

Not so well known is the mausoleum at Frogmore where the bodies of Prince Albert and Queen Victoria lie. It also is embellished with red Mull granite, supplied through MacDonald of Aberdeen,

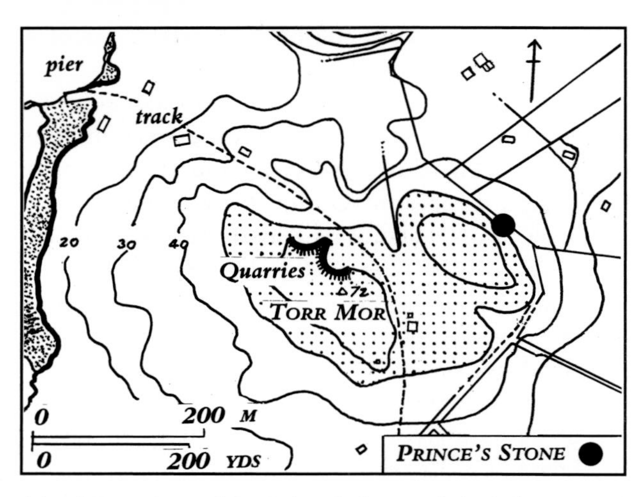

(*above*) Location of the Prince's Stone; (*below*) the monolith still in place, with part of the overlying stone removed.

and pink Mull granite from William Sim.

Roads and Bridges

Elsewhere in London there is more evidence of a link with Mull. Huge hammer-dressed blocks of granite were sent by sea and by rail to London from almost every granite quarry in Britain, including Tormore, for the building of the Thames Embankment between 1864 and 1870. The average price for granite ashlar used was 3/9 per cubic foot.

Both Westminster Bridge and Blackfriars Bridge over the Thames were built of Portland stone in the 1760s, but a hundred years later they had to be rebuilt because they were too narrow. Also, the stone below water level had been dangerously damaged by scouring and by ice. The new 1862 Westminster Bridge was of granite, some of it from Tormore.

The new Blackfriars Bridge, completed in 1869, was adorned with four spectacular 11 foot high columns of polished Tormore granite on either side. In *Granite and our Granite Industries* (1888) G.F. Harris writes: 'A good trade is done... [in Mull granite] The tremendous columns for Blackfriars Bridge were turned by a lathe now at Shap.' The machinery had probably gone to Westmoreland from Glasgow when the Shap Company took over the Mull quarries. The columns were actually turned and polished at the Glasgow Paisley Road works of the Scottish Granite Company in 1866. According to George Muir they had each been divided into three sections 'for ease of transport' and he invited the public to view the operations.

A writer in an 1868 *Journal of Agriculture* claims to have seen on Tormore pier 'some polished cylindrical blocks at least 30 tons in weight' waiting for shipment to form pillars in the new Blackfriars Bridge in London. There was never any polishing equipment in Mull. The blocks would have been roughly dressed and probably rectangular when they left the island. However, the columns were obviously famous and they can still be seen and admired today. Both Blackfriars Bridge and Holborn Viaduct were opened by Queen Victoria on 6th November 1869.

There had been fierce competition to supply finished granite for the building of Holborn Viaduct, which began in 1863. Tormore stone was selected for the twelve hexagonal supporting columns, Kemnay granite for their caps and stone from Guernsey for the bases. All were cut and polished by John Fyfe & Co. in Aberdeen, although Alexander MacDonald had been very keen to get the contract. Correspondence from both contractors survives at

Polishing the granite for Holborn Viaduct at Fyfe & Co., Aberdeen, 1868.

the City of London Records Office, as do letters discussing the enormous problems faced both in London and Aberdeen. Fortunately, George Washington Wilson photographed the special work-shop which Fyfe had set up, giving us some idea of the laborious processes involved

The polished piers ready for shipment. Both photographs by George Washington Wilson and reproduced courtesy of the Corporation of London Records Office, reference numbers HVI Box 23.1 and HVI Box 24.5.

Lighthouses

Four Scottish west coast lighthouses were built or partly built of Ross of Mull granite. They were all designed by members of the famous Stevenson family, six of whom were engineers to the Commissioners of Northern Lighthouses between 1799 and 1930.

Skerryvore

The first actual quarry on the Ross of Mull was opened by Alan Stevenson at North Bay in 1839, to provide stone for Skerryvore Lighthouse on the treacherous reef of rocks 30 miles to the west. The Duke of Argyll had given permission for stone to be taken free from any part of his estates and the deep-water inlet in the north coast of the Ross was selected. The hillside there was 'so steep as almost to deserve the name of a cliff' wrote Alan Stevenson, adding later 'I have never seen a granite quarry of equally great resources as regards both the quantity and the quality'.

The quarry was opened about 100 feet above high tide level. There were rails on longitudinal sleepers on a very steep incline to carry blocks down to a level working area where there were sheds and a smiddy. Before the quarry work actually started, housing was built on the opposite shore. This was described by Alan Stevenson as 'a range of barracks accommodating forty persons'.

From early times, even before the quarry opened, Camas (as North Bay is called locally) was a salmon fishing base and it remains so today. It has also been used since the 1950s by the Iona Community as a centre for outdoor youth activities in summer, the impressive buildings serving both purposes. Eventually, far more than forty people could be housed.

Hynish at the south-west point of Tiree, although twelve miles away, was the nearest land to Skerryvore and the most suitable place from which to supply and communicate, and at which to shape and dress the stones. Work on the rock could only be carried out in the summer and in reasonably good weather. A

Marks of the rails leading down from Camas quarry; the former quarrymen's barracks are opposite.

high wooden barrack on legs was twice erected for the men's living quarters. The first, in 1838, was destroyed by winter storms and although the second, the next year, was stronger the men were sometimes imprisoned in it for days by gales which lashed and rocked it.

During 102 days in 1838 and 1839, thirty men led by Charles Barclay and Alan Stevenson himself, who was often out on the rock, excavated a huge circular foundation pit in the hard gneiss at the highest point of the reef. Its diameter was 48 feet and its floor was made smooth and level.

The first three courses of the lighthouse were built of Tiree gneiss. The stone was so hard that it required 'four times as much labour and steel' as did granite to procure and shape. Granite is itself much harder than other building stones and tools for working it require frequent sharpening, but it was considered to be the ideal material for building lighthouses at that time. Eighteen courses of granite completed the 21 foot high solid masonry base which could be reached by pounding seas and upon which the lighthouse itself would be set.

At Hynish a harbour had to be built, plus a working area with sheds, a signalling tower and dwelling houses. These were nearly all of granite from Mull and were later to become a shore station for lightkeepers and their families and for servicing the lighthouse.

During the building period Hynish was a busy place with sometimes 150 men working all the year round. Under Alan's youngest brother, Thomas Stevenson, up to 70 stone-masons from north-east and south-west Scotland and other parts were meticulously cutting and dressing the Mull stone 'according to timber moulds'. Trial-fitting, course by course, ensured that it could be assembled on the rock without alteration.

Some quarriers at North Bay were local men, others came from other parts of Scotland and from Ireland. From Ross-shire came the young William Vass who was to become one of the best known quarrymasters in Scotland. Alan Stevenson's *Account of Skerryvore*, written in 1848, gives a detailed description of quarrying methods at that time and of how the stone was shaped and the lighthouse built.

Large masses of rock were brought down by carefully controlled explosion of gunpowder in boreholes about two and a half inches in diameter and up to 11 or even 14 foot deep. On one occasion a shot detached a 460 ton slab. Often pinches or crow-bars would suffice to lever out natural joints. Plugs and feathers were occasionally used in the quarry face as well as for splitting blocks on the floor.

Wedges hammered into slots along natural seam lines 'worked remarkably well in that rock', according to Alan Stevenson, to divide stone into blocks of about three-quarters to two and a half tons. 4,300 of these were formed between April 1839 and June 1840. Before leaving Mull, roughly dressed, they were subdivided into measured pieces one and a half inches larger all round than would be the finished building stones.

Stevenson's account also gives the reader some idea of the problems and ordeals faced and of the extraordinary courage, skill and perseverance which resulted in the lighting of the tallest and most elegant of towers in 1844 and has ensured safety for passing ships ever since. The perfection of its design and execution ensured the tower's survival, even after a

For dressing lighthouse stones, Alan Stevenson listed a mason's kit, worth £7 in the 1840s, as follows :

1 dressing hammer 16–18 lbs.
6 dressing picks 12–20 lbs
1 small handmall, about 4 lbs
3 stone axes, about 7 lbs
16 or 18 cast steel punches and chisels
1 or 2 chippers or pinchers, 2½ lbs. Eight men would share one large blocking hammer weighing 30 or 32 lbs.

Old brake drum, lying abandoned at Camas.

Quarrying tools found at Tormore.

raging internal fire on a night in 1954 destroyed everything within it and badly damaged the masonry. The lightkeepers watched from the farthest corner of the rock and were not hurt. A temporary light was set up and repair work later restored the tower, which should stand for many centuries to come.

Dhu Heartach

Ships might sail safely past Skerryvore but yet be wrecked on the treacherous Torran Rocks twenty miles to the south or on the large rock known as Dhu Heartach or as St John's Rock. The winter of 1865–66 was particularly stormy and, soon after the American schooner the *Guy Mannering* came to grief off Iona in January 1866, the local correspondent for the *North British Daily Mail* wrote: 'It is to be feared that too many such cases have occurred of late upon our coasts... abundantly proves the necessity of a lighthouse either upon St John's or Torran Rock as they have undoubtedly proved terribly disastrous to life and property'.

By the summer of 1867 work began on Dhu Heartach lighthouse, to be built in a similar way to Skerryvore. This time Alan Stevenson's younger brothers David and Thomas were responsible and Alan Brebner was the resident engineer. The granite required was quarried, shaped and directly shipped from the tidal island of Erraid at the south west tip of the Ross of Mull, fifteen miles from the isolated rock.

The working area on Erraid's substantial pier with its sheds, the nine houses and their wash-houses in walled gardens nearby were beautifully built with excellent fittings, so that outwardly they appear almost unchanged to this day. The quarry, the smiddy and the corrugated iron signal tower were not far away and a tramway system with horses took stone from the quarry to the working area. A steamer called *Dhu Heartach* was specially built on the Tyne to transport men and materials and to tow lighters in which 'the stones were packed with straw, hay or mats, sometimes in wooden frames and with the care of glass lest their accurately cut angles and edges should suffer'. On the rock were steam-powered cranes, also trucks on rails and, high on iron legs, barracks for the men.

Erraid must have been a hive of activity when Robert Louis Stevenson, Thomas's son, was there in the summer of 1870 and later he wrote a vivid account of it in *Memories and Portraits* :

> All day long there hung about the place the music of clinking tools... It was above all strange to see Erraid on the Sunday when the sound of the tools ceased and there fell a crystal quiet... men would be sauntering in their Sunday's best. ... [on other days, in fine weather] before the sun had risen from behind Ben More the tender would steam out of the bay. Over 15 sea-miles of the great blue Atlantic rollers she ploughed her way, trailing at her tail a brace of wallowing stone-lighters.

On the rock itself, operations were often hazardous for the workmen even after the iron barrack was ready for a resident squad by the third summer, in 1869. Bad weather could cut them off, sometimes for days. Mr Goodwillie, the foreman on the rock, was a fiddler whose playing often accompanied the storms and helped the men pass the long

Carting granite for Dhu Heartach on Erraid. Courtesy of the Scottish Ethnological Archive, National Museums of Scotland.

hours. The wind and waves could be ferocious, damaging equipment, toppling blocks and once sweeping clean into the sea the anvil of blacksmith John Burnie, as his granddaughter Helen MacKinnon often heard tell.

Before the end of 1871 the 132 foot tower was completed and early in 1872 the light, fuelled by paraffin, shone out for the first time. Robert Louis Stevenson considered the lighthouse to be a great and brave achievement and wondered if the thousands of tourists who had gone to Iona to be 'vaguely sentimental' over the graves of St Columba and his monks had ever given it a thought. To him it was as if, somehow, 'heroism was a cheaper commodity

Blocks for Dhu Heartach, tramway and machinery at the workyard on Erraid. Courtesy of the Scottish Ethnological Archive, National Museums of Scotland.

than it ever was before'.

After the lighthouse began operating Erraid served as a shore station for Dhu Heartach and, from 1892, for Skerryvore also when the families moved from Hynish. Between 1898 and 1952 it supported a small school for the children of the lighthouse men and a few others from the nearest Mull farms at Fidden and Cnocvuligan. In 1972 the shore station was transferred to Oban, ending a century-old link between Erraid and the lighthouses. Today the island is let by its Dutch owner to the Findhorn Community who maintain the houses and gardens in good order, almost as they were during the lighthouse days.

Lighthouse work in progress on Dhu Heartach rock. Courtesy of the Scottish Ethnological Archive, National Museums of Scotland.

Ardnamurchan

Alan Stevenson designed the Ardnamurchan lighthouse complex, built between 1846 and 1849, but his health was failing and he was not often at the building site.

Robert Hume of Gatehouse of Fleet was the contractor whose tender of £5,500 was the lowest of six and who had had 'much experience of granite masonry'. He had built the Little Ross lighthouse off the Galloway coast. Stone was to be quarried and dressed at North Bay. Hume often sailed between Ardnamurchan and Mull and many letters passed between him and Alan Stevenson.

During the winter of 1847 many of the men at

the quarry had scurvy and dysentery: 'We are badly off for medical advice and proper medicine' wrote Hume. They were victims, as were many local people, of the malnutrition that was rife following the disastrous potato blight which struck much of the West Highlands in 1846. Their diet had been mainly oatmeal with a little fish, eggs and milk but no vegetables. Stevenson arranged for a doctor from Glasgow to attend his men but of course work was delayed.

Nevertheless, by June 1847 there were '500 tons of dressed material from the Ross of Mull already on the ground' at Ardnamurchan. But financial problems mounted up, there was pressure to raise wages and two boats plus 'a good horse' were lost. The Tiree boatman, Allan McFadyen, who had been 'carrying stone for lighthouses' for nine years, wrote asking for help because he had a wife and nine children and his boat had been wrecked. He received £15 from the Commissioners of Northern Lighthouses.

By 1848 the 'tower was brought to its full height' but Robert Hume was in debt, 'destitute through no fault'. He had been away from home for three 'lost' years and his family in Galloway saw their furniture forfeited. He was writing desperate letters but it took some time for the Lighthouse Board to decide to let him have £500 in order to finish the project and to get for the causeway 'materials from North Bay... without delay, that we may vacate the quarry'.

Hyskeir

David Stevenson's son and Alan's nephew, David Alan Stevenson, was the engineer for Hyskeir lighthouse off the island of Canna. The contractors were J. MacDougall of Oban, foreman on the island was John Ross of Oban and the lighthouse was completed in 1904.

Built mainly of local freestone, the tower has a balcony and coping of red granite, probably from Tormore, purchased from the Shap Granite Company and finely treble-axed at Tobermory.

Docks & piers, millstones & milestones

Granite was sailed or towed from the Ross of Mull for building or adding to piers at nearby non-granite sites, such as Iona, Bunessan, Calgary and the Mishnish and Aros piers at Tobermory. Stone was also shipped much farther away, to be used in many larger docks and harbours including several in Glasgow, Greenock, Liverpool and New York.

It may also have been used at Port Rush in Northern Ireland. Alan Stevenson wrote to Charles Barclay at Hynish in 1844:

> I have some thoughts of using North Bay stone for the harbour works of Port Rush in Ireland. Be so good as to state, if possible by return of post... what rate per ton you would ask, or per foot, to quarry and ship at North Bay stones, say two tons weight and four and a half feet long...

Many Glasgow bridges are of Dalbeattie granite but Jamaica or Glasgow Bridge had some Mull stone inserted during widening at the end of last century. Kirklee Bridge over the Kelvin is considered by some to be the finest in the city. Largely built of red sandstone, it has two superb lofty columns of polished Tormore granite at either side of its main arch. These are of best quality stone – well worth seeing and comparing with the parapets above, which are of Peterhead granite.

There is a huge millstone at Ardnamurchan which was once at the lighthouse complex. It has a diameter of about four feet, is seventeen inches thick and is very precisely formed. Slightly smaller and more roughly cut is another round stone, now in a garden near Craignure. This one was used for many years as a mooring anchor off Craignure, after having served for some time as the base for a flagpole on the pier. Its original purpose is not known.

In 1878 Mr Allen of Aros House ordered from William Vass the granite milestones which still mark out the distance between Tobermory and Dervaig today. He paid 10/6 for each of them. There are several granite bollards on both the Mishnish and Aros piers at Tobermory. Lying on the grass near the former lies another, looking rather like a giant extracted tooth with its six foot long root exposed.

Oban Times 4 May 1878
The sloop *Proceed* is at present loading a cargo of granite at the Sound of Iona quarries for Liverpool.

Oban Times 27 August 1892
Ross of Mull – the Quarries. A large block of granite well over 2,000 cubic feet and weighing over 200 tons has been felled at Tormore quarry. The block is now being cut into columns nearly 20 foot long which are to be sent to Mexico. Mull granite has always been a favourite in the foreign markets.

(*left*) Granite millstone at Ardnamurchan; (*above*) similar rough circular stone, Craignure, Mull.

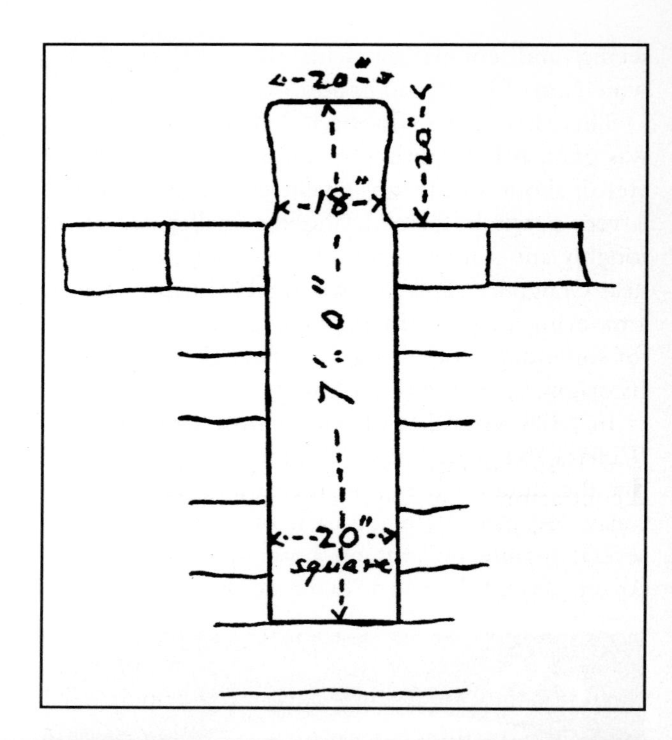

(*right*) Sketch of a mooring paul, or bollard, on a plan of the Mishnish Pier, Tobermory drawn up by D. & T. Stevenson, Engineers, 1861. (National Library of Scotland, ms. no. 5863/96)
(*below*) Granite bollard of similar design, near the Mishnish Pier, 1994.

Tormore Today

In 1986 Stewart McGlashan Limited, masonry contractors, obtained planning permission to reopen Tormore upper quarry from which stone had not been taken since 1910 and they were granted a five-year lease, renewed in 1992. Scottish Natural Stones Limited, a wholly owned subsidiary of McGlashen's, became the quarry operators and tenants of the Argyll Estate. Instead of shipping the stone from Tormore pier, the company have built a link road and lorries transport loads via the short Craignure to Oban car ferry to the company's modern works at Shotts in central Scotland. In 1994 Watson Stonecraft acquired the business.

Gone now are the hundreds of rectangular blocks, stacked almost undisturbed for most of this century. They made a spectacular landmark and viewpoint from which to look north-west to the islands between Iona and Skye. Again there is blasting from the upper quarry face, although this does not happen regularly. As of old, work depends on demand. The summer of 1990 was a busy time when a lot of granite left the island.

The blocks are no longer squared-off and quarry-dressed as they used to be for transit. Very large irregular slabs are just trimmed and only two or three of them are loaded by crane onto a long flat 38-ton articulated lorry. Each block is set down on its flattest surface and secured by wedges and ratchet chains.

There is a stark contrast between the working quarry and its long abandoned neighbour at the lower level. The two are separated by what is now a flight of rough steps on the steep slope which used to bear rails. The upper quarry is pink and sharp-edged with a flattened brown floor on which wait a few blocks with yellow numbers painted on them. A mobile crane resides and functions there, sometimes accompanied by tipper trucks, generators and other machinery worked by one or two men.

Very different is the lower quarry, green and grey with moss and lichen, mellowed by ferns, bushes, cropped grass and wild flowers. Small disused quarries can be beautiful and interesting places. Their ledges and crevices make protective homes for animals and plants. Ravens' nests or small rowan trees may occupy high corners.

In man-made cliffs and in felled rocks bore-holes

remain. Here and there rusty old plugs and feathers have been left in place, as has a jumper which still protrudes from one high face. Eventually even the few remaining bits of machinery seem to blend with nature.

In George Street, Edinburgh the headquarters of both the Trustee Savings Bank and the Sun Alliance Building Society have recently laid handsome granite floors which, not long ago, were part of Tormore. Stone has been crossing the high seas once again. Some has gone to New Zealand for the foyer and lift area of the High Commissioner's new house in Wellington. And in the Shandong province of China there is now a seven-foot high memorial of Mull granite. Commissioned by Edinburgh University, it was erected in 1991 to commemorate the life of the great Scottish Olympic athlete and missionary, Eric Liddell, who died there in 1945.

Today many people of Mull and Iona descent have connections with the quarries through members of a previous generation who worked as managers, quarrymen, stone-masons, blacksmiths or labourers. Granite has played an important role in the history and economy of the local area.

Immeasurable quantities of this fine natural resource remain at the heart of a uniquely attractive landscape. Whether much more stone will leave the island in the future we cannot tell

At the time of writing there is much debate about the possible establishment of superquarries in the west and north of Scotland, to supply anticipated demand for aggregate, mostly for road-building. Ross of Mull stone is not ideal for this purpose, however, nor is the coast suitable for the specialised modern shipping required. The closeness to Iona also makes it unlikely that quarrying other than on the present limited scale would happen here in the foreseeable future.

Polished granite is certainly very popular nowadays for cladding modern buildings, at home and abroad, as well as for headstones. It is now available from places such as India, Italy, Spain and Scandinavia, in many hues and splendid natural patterns. There is thus even more competition than there was a hundred years ago, but the rose-pink Ross of Mull granite will, it is hoped, continue to be admired and appreciated and to hold its own in today's market.

(*opposite*) Peace and natural beauty in the lower quarry at Tormore today.

Appendix

List of buildings and structures wholly or in part of Mull granite:

Lighthouses

Skerryvore
Ardnamurchan
Dhu Heartach
Hyskeir

Bridges

Blackfriars Bridge, London
Westminster Bridge, London
Holborn Viaduct, London
Jamaica or Glasgow Bridge, Glasgow
Kirklee Bridge, Glasgow

Docks, Harbours and Piers

Aros Pier, Tobermory
Mishnish Pier, Tobermory (bollards)
Bunessan Pier
Calgary Pier
Hynish Pier and harbour, Tiree
Scalasaig pier and breakwater, Colonsay
Greenock Pier & West Harbour
Glasgow Pier (coping)
Prince's Dock Sheds, Glasgow
New York Docks
Liverpool Docks
Birkenhead Docks
Barrow Docks
Thames Embankment, London

Memorials

Albert Memorial, Kensington Gardens, London
Royal Mausoleum, Frogmore, London
Cross to Duchess of Argyll, Iona
Cross to Duchess of Westminster, Loch Stack, NW Sutherland
Cailean Mòr Stone, Kilchrennan, Loch Awe
Monument to Duncan MacNeill, Lord Colonsay, Colonsay
Various headstones in graveyards at Fionnphort, Old Kilpatrick, Pennygown, Lochbuie in Mull, in Iona and Colonsay, at Pennyfuir, Oban and at Kilchrennan.

[after 1986]

Eric Liddell Memorial, China

Buildings

General Post Office, George Square, Glasgow (columns)
Trustee Savings Bank, Govan Road, Glasgow
Glasgow University (inside columns)
Argyll Car Factory, Alexandria
Dunrobin Castle, Golspie
Manchester Town Hall
St. George's Hall, Liverpool
University of Oxford Museum (polished specimen column)

[after 1986]

Halifax Building Society, Kilmarnock
Compaq Computer Facility, Erskine
Sun Alliance Offices, Edinburgh (floor)
Trustee Savings Bank, Edinburgh (floor)
High Commissioner's House, Wellington, New Zealand (foyer & lift area)

Looking north-west to the tip of Iona and the Treshnish Isles from Tormore upper level. The rectangular blocks, a reminder of the working quarry in its heyday, were removed after 1986.

Selected Sources

Davis, Keri, 'William Muir and the Blake Press at Edmonton' in *Blake An Illustrated Quarterly*, vol. 27, no. 1, (University of Rochester, summer 1993), pp. 14–25.

Harris, G.F., *Granites and the Granite Industries* (London 1888), pp. 92–95.

Kerney, Michael, 'Polished Granite in Victorian Architecture' in *Victorian Society Annual* (London 1987–88), pp. 20–32.

MacArthur, E. Mairi, Iona: *The Living Memory of a Crofting Community 1750–1914* (Edinburgh 1990).

MacCormick, John, *The Island of Mull*, 1st edn (Glasgow 1923).

Muir, George W., 'On Granite Working' in *The Practical Mechanic's Journal*, vol. II, third series, (Glasgow, Edinburgh & London, April 1866–March 1867), pp. 121–4.

Munro, R.W., *Scottish Lighthouses* (Stornoway 1979).

Robinson, Eric, 'A Geology of the Albert Memorial and Vicinity' in *Proceedings of the Geological Association*, vol. 98 (1) (1987), pp. 19–37.

Royal Commission on the Ancient and Historical Monuments of Scotland, *Argyll. An Inventory of the Monuments* vol. 3 Mull, Tiree, Coll (Edinburgh 1980); vol. 4, Iona (Edinburgh 1982).

Stanier, Peter, *Quarries and Quarrying* (Shire Album No. 134, Aylesbury 1985).

Stevenson, Alan, *Account of Skerryvore* (Edinburgh 1848).

Stevenson, Robert Louis, *Memories and Portraits* (Glasgow 1990), 1st edn 1887.

Viner, David, *The Iona Marble Quarry* (Iona 1992).

Also manuscript material from Argyll Estate Papers, National Library of Scotland, Northern Lighthouse Board letter books.